KU-496-745

FIONA HARROLD

indestructible
self-belief

7 steps to
getting it and
keeping it

PIATKUS

First published in 2005 by
Piatkus Books Ltd
5 Windmill Street
London W1T 2JA
e-mail: info@piatkus.co.uk

Text design by Briony Chappell

This book has been printed on paper manufactured
with respect for the environment using wood from
managed sustainable resources.

Data manipulation by
Action Publishing Technology, Gloucester
Printed and bound in Great Britain by
William Clowes Ltd, Beccles, Suffolk

FOR

Everyone who knows they can make their world a better place with indestructible self-belief.

Thanks to Alan Brooke at Piatkus Books for his belief and enthusiasm for *Indestructible Self-belief* and everyone at Piatkus for their hard work in getting this into its glossy finished state and into good bookshops everywhere. Thanks to Karen Swayne for her consummate editing and pulling it all together. What a trooper! Last but not least, thanks to all my clients over the years who have tried and tested everything in *Indestructible Self-belief* and shown me the power of indestructible self-belief.

Contents

1

Do you believe in you?

Whether you think you can or you think you can't, you're usually right.

HENRY FORD

The greatest asset you can have in life is indestructible self-belief. We all know that people who handle life well, achieve great things and prosper all have greater levels of self-belief than the average person. They really do. When the going gets tough Indestructible Self-Believers (ISBers) dig deep into themselves to rise up to the challenge. This is what I want for you.

I want to equip you to make the most of yourself, stretch and grow into your fullest potential. Life's easier when you believe in yourself. You feel more optimistic, more enthusiastic about everything. You're up for it. You feel there's nothing that you couldn't do, be or have, if you put your mind to it. And you have a darned fine time trying too. I guarantee that if you apply yourself, you'll finish this journey with me, feeling invigorated, uplifted and ready for anything.

Self-belief is feeling good enough. It's the feeling that you can handle what life throws at you. It's a healthy appreciation of your talents, characteristics and abilities. It's seeing yourself as special and entirely unique, like no other person on the planet. That's fabulous.

This is not about anything as superficial as looks. It goes much deeper than that. Barbra Streisand once said, 'I've been called an ugly duckling and I've been called one of the most beautiful women in the world. Go figure that.' But for someone with her levels of ISB, neither label is important. She knows that it's not what's on the surface, it's all about the confidence that comes from within. Love yourself and others will follow.

For a similar example of self-assurance in action, I give you Jennifer Lopez, often dubbed the World's Sexiest Woman. Yes, she's attractive, but so are thousands of other movie and pop wannabes, and she's in no doubt as to what gives her such extreme allure. 'Being sexy comes from being confident,' she says. 'People who are OK with themselves are the sexiest.' So rather than despairing that you don't have JLo's curves, love the body you have. (And if you don't love the way you look right now, then do something about it!) But most importantly, focus on what's great about you. It could be your fabulous sense of humour, your generous heart, your fearlessness, or your ability make others feel at ease. Whatever it is, that's the real secret of being attractive to others. Being happy with yourself brings a self-assurance that is compelling and charismatic.

Think of it this way: life is a confidence trick. With enough confidence, you can get away with anything. Real confidence is the unshakeable conviction that the world is unfolding to your advantage and that you can handle anything life throws at you, that you'll always find a way through, because there's always a way – and you'll find it. It's a blend of optimism, charm and energy. Sometimes it's sheer chutzpah and downright bluff as you talk yourself up, psyche yourself up and push yourself out of the door to convince others of your worth and abilities, knowing that the more convinced you are, the more they will be. And it's something worth striving for, because trying to get through life without confidence is a whole lot harder than it is with confidence.

We all gravitate towards confident, self-assured individuals. They're magnetic, more energetic, more uplifting, more optimistic. That feeling rubs off on those around them and you leave them feeling boosted by their brightness and outlook. It's no wonder that they tend to attract more opportunities and good fortune than the average person. These are the people envied for their 'charmed lives'.

➤ Don't belittle yourself

Obvious really, so why would anyone want to make life harder for themselves? You'd be surprised. It might not be intentional, but constant self-criticism can actually turn you into the kind of person you're desperate not to be. So be aware of the relationship between your thoughts and how you behave. If you constantly belittle yourself, or tell yourself you're not good enough, you'll start behaving in a way that reinforces that thought pattern. But if you tell yourself you are talented and special, you'll behave in a way that fulfils this belief.

➤ *There's always another level*

However tough and resilient you think you are right now, there's always another level to take yourself to. Indestructible self-belief means that whatever happens you have the internal resources to recover fast and fully. You're tough, supple and agile. You're indomitable, irrepressible. You could never be defeated, whatever happened. The bigger the challenge, the setback or letdown, the more you pull out of yourself. A crisis never leaves you where it finds you because you're sharper and taller afterwards. You're awesome, indestructible. I came across a fabulous example of this type of indestructible self-belief recently from a talk given in 1998 by Bill Gates, the billionaire owner of Microsoft. He was talking to a group of business students and was asked by one of them what he would do if he lost everything, his wealth, his business, everything. He paused for a moment and said, 'starting another company like that again, I'd have a bash doing it.' This is the answer of someone with no fear and phenomenal self-assurance. This is precisely the sort of feeling that you want to have within yourself. In my experience, it's incredibly rare as the average person is plagued by self-doubt and insecurity. Decide right now to engender this same demeanour of a Bill Gates rather then fall in with the norm.

➤ Prize yourself

You may not know the name of Vira Hladun-Goldmann. But she made history in 1998 when she won America's largest divorce settlement – a cool $44 million. After 33 years by her husband's side, helping, advising and supporting him as he built up his banking career, she felt it was her due. 'I would have been well off if I'd accepted a quarter or a tenth of the money, but it's not in my nature to do that,' she said. 'To me, marriage meant partnership and I was entitled to half. And no one was going to take it away from me.' Now there's a lady with a sense of self-belief that's as big as her bank balance!

➤ *Freshen up*

Look around you. You'll see two types of people. One has a defeated look. Life has taken its toll and they've sunk under the weight of it all. It shows in their faces. The other type is the undefeated. They look fresh. They've kept themselves light. They've had their fair share of challenges. But it's their handling of themselves and their challenges that's made the difference. They haven't allowed themselves to be ground down, worn out. They're refused to resign or give up. They've never given up – on themselves. I saw this at a young age growing up in Northern Ireland. As a daddy's girl I spent vast amounts of time with my dad and he just happened to be a self-improvement fanatic. We were full-time people-watchers and nothing gave me more fun than driving around County Armagh on summer evenings picking up hitch-hikers. These unsuspecting travellers would be my 'client' for the duration of the journey as I delicately questioned them about their lives, their perspective and feelings about everything that had ever happened to them and their expectations about the future. What I heard and saw then was that those individuals with healthy self-belief were more resilient and able to bounce back from life's inevitable challenges, while those without it sank under the weight of it all, looking burdened and ground down. This is true today, more than 25 years later. All of our outlook and interpretation of *everything* that happens to us is down to us. Life is a spin. I don't mean that to sound superficial, but it's our *interpretation* of life and all that happens that gives it its meaning.

The Brazilian writer Paolo Coelho, author of the bestselling work *The Alchemist*, was imprisoned and tortured for his political beliefs but, rather than feeling bitter, he believes his experiences have helped him appreciate the moment. 'It's a matter of attitude,' he says, 'of believing that every day contains our past and future lives. So we must relax, and enjoy and respect every day. If I had to have an epitaph it would be: "he died alive", because there are people who appear to have died much earlier than their actual death.'

Coelho's perspective has been shaped by events which few of us can imagine. An angry young radical, he was a popular spokesman against the military dictatorship in his country, until one night he was ambushed by three men with guns as he walked home with his wife. 'They threw me onto the grass. Someone cocked a gun and I was sure he was going to shoot. I looked at this beautiful sky full of stars and I thought: "I am going to die at 26. I didn't live my life."' His life was spared, but the experience left a lasting impact. 'Since then, I have never felt in total control of my life. And I'm glad, it was a most important lesson,' he says. 'You don't control anything. You can be the most successful author, and then you cross the street and you're dead. Tragedy can wait for you around any corner. So now I take every day as a miracle. Carpe diem, seize the day, because nothing can guarantee you are going to see another sunrise. Only when I understood that did I find the strength to move on.'

This is the type of resilience that I have in mind for you. Don't worry if you think you've become a little defeated yourself. As long as you're willing, we can handle that. You can freshen up in no time. And, even if you already see yourself as an Indestructible Self-Believer (ISBer), you'll want to run a check to ensure you're firing on all cylinders.

➤ *Get clear*

Right now, I want you to get absolutely clear what your current level of self-belief is. Ask yourself whether there's a figure that springs to mind, a percentage between 0 and 100% that sums up your general feeling of self-belief. Don't worry if a figure doesn't immediately occur to you. What I want you to do now is identify that level in the principal areas of your life. One could be your professional life and career, others could be your personal life, your social groups or relationships. Don't linger over this. Just go with the figure that immediately comes to mind. It might be surprising to notice that you have high self-belief in one area but much less in another. No matter. It's all going to increase from now on anyway.

THE WORK

1 Buy a new notebook. Carry it with you at all times so you can jot down observations and insights.

2 Choose an area of your life that you want to focus ➤

➤ on to increase your self-belief. Be absolutely clear what your current level is. Write this down at the back of your notebook with today's date next to it.

3 Write down this heading, *What this lack of self-belief has cost me.* It's vital that you grasp the damage that low self-belief has done so far. Keep this line of enquiry open for the rest of the week and add to it as things occur to you. Now write down another heading, *The difference it would make to my life if I doubled my self-belief would be . . .*

This is where the fun starts! Allow yourself to begin to get excited at the prospect of leaving behind some out-of-date thinking about yourself and shedding a few self-imposed limitations.

4 Live one day at a time as if you really did have double the amount of self-belief. Every morning put on the mantle, the demeanour of someone with double of amount of self-belief in that aspect of your life. What would change? Looking at you, how would I know you'd just doubled your quota, your level? Would you appear more relaxed, ➤

➤ approachable? friendly, confident, happy? Make a list and do a few things that you might not have done previously. Have fun with this. It's not hard work!

5 Study other ISBers. In public life, there are the obvious ones – Madonna, whose mother died of breast cancer when she was just five, but who has never seen herself as a victim. With willpower and talent she turned herself into the biggest star on the planet. Or Sharon Stone, who has fought back from a brain haemorrhage and divorce, and still exudes optimism, glamour and charisma. She isn't afraid to attack the age-ism she sees in Hollywood producers. 'When women hit 40 in Hollywood, they get punished,' she declares. 'We Barbie dolls are not meant to behave the way I do,' she says. 'To be a good role model, you have to be willing to fail in public.'

Moral: High expectations are the key to everything.

2
What's your opinion of you?

I'm not the average girl from your video. And I ain't built like a supermodel. But I learned to love myself unconditionally.

INDIA ARIE, from the song 'Video'

In this chapter, we're going to look closely at how you see yourself. What's your take on you? How do you rate your potential? I'm going to show you how to ensure that you have the highest possible regard for yourself.

Now you've assessed your self-belief levels in the various areas of your life, it's time to take action. Don't worry one iota if you've identified a low percentage in one or more areas. You're here to upgrade and upgrade you will.

I want to impress upon you the absolute necessity of building strong self-belief and ensure that your opinion of yourself is pristine and powerful. A strong foundation of self-belief is the basis on which to build an interesting life. Without it, you could be tempted to scale down your aspirations and ambitions, giving into fear and self-doubt, without ever testing yourself in the first place. As I write this, the brilliant young British actor, Toby Stephens is playing Hamlet to rave reviews and packed houses in a London theatre. I laughed when I read his comment on his current career success, 'One of the many bum things about being an actor is you can never be sure that anyone's going to want you. Can you imagine going up for job interviews once or twice a week and being rejected nine times out of 10? That's the trickiest part of the job – you've got to have insane self-belief to withstand that.' How right he is, and the life of a jobbing actor certainly does require extraordinary levels of self-belief, not just when they're in work, but all the other times when they're not.

➤ *The ultimate advantage*

Modern ISBers are the new elite. They belong to a club that is open to anyone. You can join any time you're ready to do a little work on yourself and maintain that elevated status.

Are great self-believers made or born? Can anyone be one? There can be no doubt that having self-belief instilled in you from an early age is a huge advantage. Research suggests that people who have had a happy childhood with their mothers are more likely to grow up to be effective leaders. Having a parent or authority figure implant and nurture your self-belief as you are still forming so it is woven into the very fabric of your being builds a phenomenal powerhouse.

Singer-songwriter Daniel Bedingfield became an overnight star when his single, 'Gotta Get Thru This' – recorded in his bedroom at his parents' home with just a computer and a microphone – reached No. 1 when he was 21. The country has many talented young musicians, so what was it which helped propel him out of his bedroom and onto *Top of the Pops*? He credits his family. 'I have really good role models in my parents and my mum and dad have always given me the most amazing support,' he says. 'They've always believed in my talent – in fact, they think I'm better than I am.'

Typecasting a child in a negative role can also be a self-fulfilling prophecy. Child psychologists have long warned of the dangers of pigeonholing youngsters, pointing out that if you don't want your son or daughter to behave badly, it makes sense not to go around telling everyone what a nightmare they are.

But while low expectations lead to low self-esteem and low achievements, the opposite is also true. More than 30 years ago, a study demonstrated that if you tell people what to expect of the children they are dealing with, the end results will be affected by that information. The research project gave teachers enhanced expectations of their pupils' performance and found that the youngsters performed better than would have been expected. No surprise really.

This labelling happens all the time in families. How many times have you heard a parent describe one of their children as 'the bright one' (making, by definition, other siblings 'not so bright') or 'the lazy one' (why would they even bother to try to change)?

Parental expectations can be so high that even the brightest children feel like failures if they don't achieve straight As in their exams. And the sense that they have disappointed their parents and teachers can linger into adulthood, found a survey by the University of London's Institute of Education. They interviewed hundreds of youngsters who were considered 'academically promising' when they started secondary school, and followed them up in their mid-20s to see if they had 'fulfilled their potential'. They'd all achieved various levels of success in their chosen fields, but what was really interesting was their response to their achievements, and how that early pressure stayed with them. A significant minority considered themselves failures because they had not met parental expectations.

➤ *Emotional support*

Emotional support, not pressure, is the key. There is now clear evidence that children with higher self-esteem at ten get as much of a boost to their adult earning power as those with higher maths or reading ability. This crucially comes from the home, but for some lucky children an inspirational teacher can make all the difference.

Blackwell Primary School in the old mining village of Alfreton, Derbyshire, had well below average scores, and expectations for the children were low when Delyth Girdler became head in 1998. Four years later, there was such a turnaround, the school emerged as the most improved year on year, something the headmistress puts down to raising the children's self- esteem. 'The biggest thing we had to counter is low expectations of what a child can achieve,' said Mrs Girdler. 'Many of the children come from homes where education isn't necessarily a priority, and where they don't have access to books, so we need to show them how good they are.'

An inner-city school which became notorious for all the wrong reasons is St George's, the west London comprehensive where the head teacher Philip Lawrence was murdered. When 'superhead' Marie Stubbs was brought in to try to restore order, her first act was to shake hands with every pupil. 'Every child should be intrinsically valued,' she said. That approach, combined with a 'zero tolerance' policy on behaviour and appearance, and the visits of positive role models from the world of sport and entertainment made such a huge difference that, after months of hard work, St George's was removed from Ofsted's failing list and pronounced 'a good school'.

Marie Stubbs' methods mirror those of schools in Ghana, which are getting such good results from their pupils that parents in England are even sending their sons and daughters to Africa to learn. Lacking role models and held back by low expectations, black children in Britain lag badly behind their white and Asian peers. One boy whose despairing family sent him to Ghana recalls that in London, 'no-one at school had any ambition. If you ask kids in Ghana what they want to be, they say pilots, neurosurgeons, lawyers. In London the kids just shrug and say, "I dunno". That means they're heading for the bottom.' Another said, 'Here in Ghana everyone wants to succeed. It's not cool or clever to fail.'

➤ *Taking control of your life*

The story of Pav Akhtar is a lesson in how taking control of your life can change your destiny. Akhtar, the first ethnic minority president of the Cambridge University Students' Union, put himself into council care at 14 to escape family problems. One of five children, he was born in Preston, the son of Pakistani parents. His father was a lorry driver, his mother a disabled housewife who spoke no English. He said after his election that he hoped his story would be an inspiration for other ethnic minority students and children from care homes who dream of making it to Oxbridge. 'I had quite a tough childhood,' he recalled. 'I knew the right thing to do was to move out of that environment. My parents were against me going into care. It's not what a good Asian kid does.' But he persisted, and spent two years in a children's home, while continuing at school. After studying A levels in night school while working in the day to finance his studies, he gained a place at Cambridge University. 'My parents are extremely proud of me and what I have achieved. My father had thought I was doomed because I put myself into care and it would be extremely bad for me. I challenge the stereotype since you can't write people off.'

The effects of low academic success or poverty can both be overcome with self-belief. Cherie Blair grew up in a relatively poor single-parent household with little academic background, but significant emotional support from her mother Gale. Her father, the actor Tony Booth, walked out on the family when Cherie was only five. She saw little of him, but worked hard at school, got herself into the London School of Economics, where she out-classed all her more privileged contemporaries. She is now one of Britain's most distinguished barristers, as well as being the wife of the Prime Minister.

The Virgin entrepreneur Richard Branson left school at 16 with mediocre qualifications and was also dyslexic. However, he came from an affluent and encouraging upper middle-class family, his mother and grandmother both famously supportive. He went on to become one of the 20 richest men in Britain. High levels of self-esteem and self-belief are what have given him the edge.

➤ *Smashing the class barriers*

Poverty is truly no barrier to being a high achiever – in a poll of the 70,000 millionaires in Britain, over half came from poor backgrounds. Today, the class barriers which held back previous generations have been well and truly smashed and anyone can rise to the top. Some predict there has been such a reversal that a privileged upbringing can even be seen as a hindrance. Fifty years ago, an education at Eton was a guaranteed golden future for the lucky few. But now the top public school is no longer a passport to success. And for many true self-believers, lack of education never stood in their way.

The self-made multi millionaire Sir Alan Sugar started life as the son of a poverty-stricken East End tailor. Growing up in a two-bedroom council flat in Hackney, he vowed to escape the poverty of his childhood. He started young, coming up with money making schemes from an early age. After a brief spell in an office, he struck out on his own, forming Amstrad. A tough, shrewd businessman with an unnerving eye for gaps in the market, he made a fortune from his electronic empire, bringing affordable computers to the British public. Now worth a reputed £700 million, he declares bluntly 'I will not allow anything in my life to fail.'

Growing up dyslexic in the 50s was a start in life which would challenge even the strongest characters, and David Bailey recalls how teachers at his East London school predicted he would be a failure. 'They treated me like an idiot and said I would never make anything of myself,' he remembers. Undeterred, he pursued his passion for photography and by 22 was working for *Vogue*. His name is now synonymous with some of the most iconic images of the past 40 years, but he's never forgotten those who wrote him off as a child. When he was awarded the CBE in 2001, he described the honour as 'one in the eye' for those teachers who had such little faith in him.

Like Bailey, you may not have received the best possible psychological input as you were growing up. No matter. All the more incentive to make up for it now. The truth is you can grow your own self-belief any time you decide. I am going to act as your coach in this regard. Whether you're after a massive kick-start to upgrade your self-belief or a gentle boost, my tried-and-tested techniques really work. Awareness is 50% of the battle.

Waking up to the need for greater self-belief, alerting yourself to its power takes you to the halfway line.

➤ *What do you want to believe?*

What do you want to believe about you? The truth is you can believe anything you want. Whatever you *choose* to believe will be true for you in your life, because that's the view that you'll feed and cleave to. You'll accumulate evidence to prove your position, because that's simply what we humans do. We have a need to be right, so whatever we believe, whatever that perspective is, like a heat-seeking missile, we'll locate the evidence to prove our position. So, it's best to be clear what you want to be right about, because that will shape your experience of life and your opinion on – you.

I was reminded of this only last week at a dinner party when the host was talking about Sarah, his 53-year-old recently divorced neighbour. He lamented the fact that although she was wonderfully vivacious and glamorous and ran a successful estate agency, she'd find it virtually impossible to find a boyfriend at that age. Everyone around the table nodded knowingly in agreement. I asked him why he believed this to be the case when she was such a sensational person in every way. He explained that no man of 53 would be interested in her, preferring a much younger woman and Sarah would not be interested in a toy boy younger man, so she was stuck. Is this true? Absolutely.

If Sarah believes it, this will be her reality, all that she will see, expect and look for. Is it true for everyone? Absolutely not. Just the day before I'd met 64-year-old Jibby Beane who relaunched her life after divorce at 50, moving from the family home to a loft apartment in London's East End. Jibby's self-esteem and self-belief is such that it genuinely wouldn't occur to her that men wouldn't find her attractive, whatever their age. Her current paramour is 37. I am not for one moment saying that all 50-something women should aim to have a younger boyfriend or that this is the best indication of their self-esteem. I'm saying that one should have enough self-regard not to rule out any chap finding you attractive. Do you want the beliefs and outlook of a Sarah or a Jibby? Consider how attractive one is with sky high chutzpah, safe in the knowledge of her own value and the other who is 'realistic' and expects next to nothing. Who do you think is the most magnetic and charismatic, even though she is 14 years older?

➤ How upbringing boosts self-belief

Singer and songwriter Dido has topped the album and singles charts, selling millions and becoming one of the few British pop acts to make an impression on the American market. But she says success hasn't changed her as a person, because her belief in herself has always been rock solid. 'I used to work in Cafe Flo in Islington,' she says, 'but even as a waitress I didn't feel any less special than I do now.' She attributes this unshakeable self-confidence to her upbringing. 'I had complete freedom,' she recalls. 'The only rule I remember was not to lie. Dad always made me feel really beautiful. I don't have some weird self-esteem issue; that would be exhausting.'

Compare Dido's remarkable self-assurance to the revelation that most women feel depressed when looking at pictures of supermodels. Worse, the images of flawless models have an almost instantaneous effect on the way ordinary women feel, with tests showing it takes just one to three minutes for most women to feel dissatisfied with their looks.

➤ *You are far smarter and resourceful than you think*

Now that you're a grown-up, the most important influence in your life is you. This gives you an awesome power to influence yourself. You have the power to be your greatest ally or your most deadly enemy. Which is it to be? Enhancing your self-belief begins with a decision, the decision to reappraise your view of yourself, so that you enjoy the advantage of exceptional self-belief.

THE WORK

1 What is your opinion of you? Is it good enough?
Could you think better of yourself? Where could you
enhance it? The key to a real, enduring upgrade is to
back up your enhanced appreciation with hard
evidence. Remember: you have to convince you.
Whatever new perspective you want to absorb about
yourself, find compelling evidence to convince
yourself of the genuine truth underneath your new
belief. For your new belief to ring true, you must be
able to validate it for yourself. If you want to see
yourself as a sharp thinker, look into your life, past
and present, to show you justify such a belief. What
are the three key beliefs that, if you truly believed
them to be true, would make the most significant
improvement to your life? Note these down right
now. Take one at a time and identify the evidence
that already exists in your life to justify such a belief.
You're looking for evidence to make it easier for you
to believe and strengthen that belief.

2 Choose to be a 'Believer in You' from this day forth.
Don't wait for anyone else to show faith. Declare ➤

WHAT'S YOUR OPINION OF YOU? **29**

➤ backing for yourself right now. Announce it to
yourself and no one else.

3 What difference will this backing mean to you, in
your life? Make a list. What difference would you like
it to make? What's going to change in you and your
life? Get absolutely clear. Isn't that exciting? It should
be! Otherwise, think again.

4 Surround yourself with the right people. There is
absolutely no value in spending time with detractors.
We all need good people in our lives, people who
are on our side. Think very carefully about your
team, the people closest to you, that you listen to
and spend time with. If you have positioned people
close to you who will make it difficult for you to
think highly of yourself and move forward in life,
decide what you want to do about this.

5 Take yourself out to lunch! Or buy yourself a
massage – come on, don't make any of this into
hard work. I want you to enjoy the process. Take it
seriously by all means, but lighten up too. You're on
the right track, asking quality questions,   ➤

➤ challenging yourself, checking your actions. Pat yourself on the back. ISBers would do this. Honestly – they'd do it instinctively, automatically.

Moral: Know in your heart that you are far bigger than anything that can happen to you.

3

Take responsibility

I don't think of myself as a poor deprived ghetto girl who made good. I think of myself as somebody who, from an early age, knew I was responsible for myself and I had to make good.

OPRAH WINFREY

So far you've been exploring your relationship with you and grasping the critical importance of robust self-belief. You now know that the most powerful and influential person in your life is you. You are the thinker of your thoughts. You have ultimate responsibility, the final say in defining who you are and how your life is. In particular, you have sole responsibility for choosing your response to any and every situation in your life, past, present and future.

Oprah Winfrey rose from poverty and a troubled youth to become the most powerful and influential woman in television and the US. Her talk show is the highest rated in TV history and through smart business decisions she's created a raft of magazines and websites which have made her the first African-American female billionaire. It's a phenomenal triumph for anyone, let alone a black woman who was born to teenage parents in rural Mississippi. Raised until she was six by her grandmother, Oprah then moved back with her mother, to a life of hardship and sexual abuse. Rebelling by experimenting with drugs and sex, at 14 Oprah gave birth to a stillborn baby. These experiences could have destroyed her life, but instead she has used them to empower others, working her way up from presenting the news on local radio to create a global media empire. She's never blamed or looked to others to make sense of her traumatic past. 'I'm surprisingly healthy, mentally healthy. I never internalised sexual abuse as this awful thing that had happened to me. I'm neither guilty nor angry.'

I want to coach you to take greater responsibility for yourself, to take full ownership of your attitude and mental approach to life. You can't always be in control of what happens in life but you can always be in control of your response. It's entirely up to you to assign meaning and significance to events and circumstances.

In his extraordinary book, *Man's Search for Meaning*, Victor Frankl talks of his experience in a concentration camp. 'We who lived in concentration camps can remember the men who walked through the huts comforting others, giving away their last piece of bread; they offered sufficient proof that everything can be taken away from a man but one thing, the last of the human freedoms, to choose one's attitude in any given set of circumstances, to choose one's own way.'

➤ *It's all down to you*

Thankfully, few of us will be tested in the extreme way that Frankl and many others were or indeed many continue to be around the world today. Your everyday life and the challenges it brings give you ample scope for training and refining your mental outlook.

The first place to start in taking greater responsibility for you and your life is with your parents. The people you're most likely to blame for anything, and I mean *anything* you're not entirely satisfied with, are your mother and father. For some, the challenges are particularly tough, but that doesn't mean you can't still choose your response to even the cruellest upbringing.

The singer-songwriter Seal recalls the effect his tough childhood has had on him. Abandoned at birth and cared for in a foster family until he was four, he was taken back by his violent father. But instead of allowing the years of beatings to ruin his life, Seal used it to spur him onto success. 'My experiences as a child ingrained in me a survival mechanism and now I'm a very optimistic person. I always look for the light at the end of the tunnel – even if that light is so faint you can barely see it,' he says. 'My father could not see when life was good. I could be like him but I know I never will, because I see what all that anger, bitterness and negativity does to you in the end.'

Martin Seligman from the University of Pennsylvania has concluded in his 30 years' work researching depression that, crucially, it's how we regard events from our past which determine our present happiness. 'Insufficient appreciation and savouring of the good events in your past, and overemphasis of the bad ones, are the two culprits that undermine serenity, contentment and satisfaction.'

➤ *The blame culture*

The blame culture is all pervasive. After parents, it's school, friends, boyfriend, girlfriend, husband, wife. The truth is that people can hurt each other no matter how much love they share. There is no mythical partner or parent who will never hurt or disappoint. But by coming to terms with the concept of forgiveness, you can make allowances for human frailties and start the healing process.

For some people, there's always someone to blame for something. Britain in particular has a reputation as a moan and blame culture. American Express commissioned a survey recently, which reported that a staggering 52% of UK respondents wanted to fundamentally change their lives. Their excuse for not doing so: they couldn't find the time!

➤ *What do you want?*

Whether it's the readers of self-help books, too busy reading to take action or the many people who feel stuck and trapped in their lives, feeling helpless and lost, the notion of being able to choose a better life seems fanciful. The simple question, what do you want? throws them into a blind panic.

In a recent survey of 2,300 Britons, 57 per cent said given the chance of rewriting history, they would choose a different job. But how many will actually do anything about it? With low levels of self-belief, not many. But with high levels of self-belief, anything is possible!

As a coach, a vital part of my job is to spot excuses and highlight how and where my clients can take greater responsibility for their results. I want to do the same for you now. I want to challenge you to turn up your responsibility radar, so you're acutely sensitive to your attitude and responses to everything. I want you to identify how and where you might give power away to outside forces. Do you ever blame the weather, dark nights and the onset of winter for feeling flat? Resist! Taking responsibility in this instance could mean doing one of the following:

1 Buying a light box to provide some artificial daylight

2 Taking St John's Wort to boost your serotonin levels

3 Doing more aerobic exercise to activate feel-good hormones

4 Booking a holiday in the sun

5 Planning a move to a sunnier clime

➤ *You have choices*

You could add to this list. But you take my point. I'm inviting you to rid yourself of any tendency to moan or blame anyone or anything for your mood, mental outlook or situation in life. Otherwise, you're inadvertently giving away your power of response to some outside force; seeing yourself as less than completely capable, totally in charge of your life. How very uninspiring that would be.

The reason people moan is that they feel they have no choice. They convince themselves that they're powerless, and see themselves as victims. Never, ever do yourself the disservice of thinking like this. You always have choices. Practise seeing choices everywhere you look, for yourself and for others. Remind yourself that staying stuck and complaining is a choice in itself, however covert.

Women, in particular, need to run regular checks on our psyches to ensure we are not guilty of the Cinderella complex, whereby we're secretly waiting to be saved by our very own Prince Charming! This conditioning runs very deep. You might even think being a bit hopeless and hapless is endearing. Not any more. Times have changed. Modern girls take total responsibility for their own happiness, financial stability and fulfilment. Relationships work better that way.

This notion of self-reliance is in tune with the times. Being unmarried no longer means being labelled as left on the shelf. Twenty years ago marriage was a girl's only goal – even for the brightest female university graduates. Now, increasing numbers of people are choosing to live on their own, people are delaying marriage and children, singletons are on the rise and divorce is up. Instead of treating this as a national crisis, look at it this way:

perhaps more people are deciding that staying in a restrictive and unfulfilled relationship is no longer an option. True love is a wonderful thing, but so is self-sufficiency and independence. Being self-reliant is something to be saluted, not despaired of. So celebrate your independence and equality and ensure you're not waiting to be rescued. Get off to that ball yourself! Don't wait to be asked.

➤ The science of happiness

How many times have people told you to look on the bright side? They have a point. Instead of endlessly dwelling on negative images from the past, and reliving moments when things went wrong, change your focus and recall the good times instead. Experience the sense of pleasure which comes from a memory of a wonderful time and your spirits will lift. Regularly counting our blessings, rather than our burdens, have been proven to improve our mood, performance and relationships.

Another well-worn phrase is that laughter is the best medicine, and guess what? Modern medical findings are confirming this is true! Studies of individuals who live to over 100 has shown that most share a lively sense of humour, with researchers concluding that humour is a good indicator of how flexible and creative the person is in dealing with life's challenges.

A good sense of humour can also bring amazing health benefits. A study at Indiana State University in the US found that roaring with laughter can boost the immune system by an amazing 40%. Scientists took samples of the immune cells from two groups of healthy women, one who'd watched a comedy video, the other who'd watched a dull video on tourism, and mixed them with cancer cells to see how effectively they attacked the disease. They found that the women who had found the comedy funny enough to laugh out loud had significantly healthier immune systems afterwards than those who had watched the tourism film.

Going hand in hand with laughter is being happy with your life. Many experts now believe that contentment is the key to good health. Research on heart patients has shown that the quality of a person's marriage can help predict their recovery from surgery. A good marriage can give someone a reason to fight back to health, while those with a bad marriage were up to eight times more likely to die within four years. Of course we can't all conjure up a happy marriage out of thin air, but we can do much to lower our stress levels by checking our outlook, and choosing to be optimistic. Happiness is often a choice about how you respond to a given event, so choose your responses carefully.

A similar conclusion was reached by scientists from Boston University. They discovered that hostility is a better predictor of heart disease than the traditional risk factors of unhealthy living, with incidences of coronary heart disease more common in those with higher levels of hostility than those with high choles- terol, alcohol intake or even smoking tobacco.

➤ *Grow younger*

With people living increasingly long lives, experts predict that living to 100 will soon be commonplace. The astonishing increases in life expectancy have seen the typical male life spans go from 48 in 1901 to 75 in 2000, and female from 49 to 80.

And this could rise even higher as researchers continue

to make breakthroughs into the science of ageing. We'll not only live longer, we'll be healthier too.

➤ *Age better*

In 2003, as younger rivals saw their shows being axed, Des O'Connor became at the age of 71 the highest-paid presenter in Britain with his £3.7 million deal with ITV for just 12 months' work. The showbiz veteran also became a father again at 72.

It's all to do with spirit and attitude, not age. Today's 30-somethings refuse to give up their old lifestyles, spending their money on the best clothes, holidays, clubs and restaurants. They've kept their curiosity, they're still open-minded. And as for middle age, forget it. Forty is no longer frumpy – think *Sex and the City*'s Kim Cattrell, Madonna, Nigella Lawson.

The two main peaks in population are 30–44-year-olds and 45 to 55-year-olds, thanks to the baby booms of the 1960s and post Second World War. They're a powerful economic force, with advertisers waking up to the fact that they can't afford to ignore the 40-plus market. But while there's no such thing as a typical 45-year-old, what they do share is a thirst for discovery and experience. They're healthier, wealthier and more style conscious than ever before, and they still treat life as an adventure.

Then there are the over-50s who are escaping the rat race for adventure holidays, or by taking early retirement and heading overseas. Today's gap year traveller is as likely to be a stressed-out executive or pensioner as a pre-university student. With their mortgages paid off, and money in the bank, they're travelling the world, using some of the capital they've worked hard for to have some fun, instead of passing it all on to their children. There's a great name for this – SKI-ing (Spending the Kids' Inheritance)!

Saga, the travel group for the over-50s, reports that adventurous destinations are becoming more and more popular, as their holiday makers choose exotic destinations like Nepal, Vietnam and Cambodia.

For some, the experience is a catalyst for a complete lifestyle change, for others, simply an unforgettable experience.

By 2007, for the first time, there will be more Britons aged over 65 than there will be children under 16. Some see this as a demographic time bomb, but why should it be? Financially independent, and wanting to have fun, they don't intend to settle for conventional retirement.

How about the fabulous Joan Collins as an example of how to age in style? It's not always easy for great beauties to accept the passing of the years, so who could not have cheered as, in her late 60s, she exuded enviable style, pictured lounging on a yacht in bikini and shades with Percy Gibson, the husband half her age, by her side. Joan shows no sign of settling for early nights in with a cup of cocoa, and why should she, when her energy, lust for life and glamour keep her so eternally youthful?

The same applies to those other great survivors, the Rolling Stones. The legendary rock'n'roll band show no sign of taking things easy, even after a 40-year career. Both Mick Jagger and Keith Richards celebrated turning 60 on the road in the middle of their latest world tour (their 190th!). The band are rich enough for the incentive of money to be a distant memory. No, what drove them was 'fun' according to 56-year-old guitarist Ronnie Wood. It was a love of music which brought them together in the first place, they've been living out their passion every day of their lives, and that love has never died. With their drug-taking days behind them, they're fit and as lithe and lean as they ever were. So what if they have a few more grooves in those famous faces? Talk of their retirement is missing the point – making music is what they do, so why stop now when they still get such a kick out of it?

➤ Get spiritual

Brain scans of devout Buddhists have found exceptional activity in a spot called the left pre-frontal lobe, which is associated with positive emotions and good moods. In people who are depressed, angry or stressed, the right frontal cortex is more active.

Are all Buddhists born with a 'happy gene'? Unlikely, to say the least. No, these findings would seem to suggest that there is something in their lifestyle which brings them contentment.

But do you have to commit to a life of orange robes and

meditation to train yourself to be happy? Well, that's one answer. But this is not just about religion. Calming the mind is a habit we can all develop. Striving to rid ourselves of ignorance, hatred and greed is something we can all do in our everyday lives.

Think of the delight a child takes in discovering the world around them. As adults, we lose that innocent optimism and tend to focus on what's bad. As Dr Rowan Williams, Archbishop of Canterbury says, 'we have stopped being surprised. We look at one another with boredom and anxiety rather than expectant joy.'

Whatever your spiritual beliefs, you can choose to opt out of the consumer lifestyle which leaves us so ultimately unfulfilled. Constantly striving to have the latest designer outfit, state-of-the-art television or top-of-the-range car is a self-defeating exercise. Whatever we have, there will always be something we don't have. I'm not advocating giving away all your possessions, just that you be aware that contentment doesn't come from material goods.

Shopping can't give us what we truly need most because ultimately it doesn't provide the fulfilment that it promises. Gripped by shopping fever and the need to impress, we have less time to consider anything else, let alone thinking about living the best and most meaningful life possible.

THE WORK

1 Let it go! Eradicate all blame from your perspective. Choose to see the benefit in all your circumstances, however gruesome.

Revisit anything you feel ambivalent or regretful about, be it the school you went to, the area you grew up in, the peer pressure you were exposed to. See the potential for benefit in all of it. The end goal is to achieve a feeling of gratitude for all of it as you turn it all to your advantage.

Remember: if it didn't kill you, it could make you stronger. The choice is yours.

2 Watch your language. Your attitude is revealed in your choice of words. Be on the lookout for any ➤

➤ indications of victim-speak. You are reinforcing mental habits in your choice of words, so only speak of that which you want to bring about. Build yourself up with words of encouragement, patience and inspiration. Avoid knocking yourself with defeatist or demeaning messages.

3 Don't moan. About anything or anyone. It's a bad habit, it's addictive and it's a slippery slope to an overall malaise. Train yourself to just not do it. You can change your view of your reality or change the reality itself. Choose your tactic and make it work.

4 Develop gratitude. Adopt an attitude of gratitude towards yourself. You're fortunate to have the talents, abilities and vision that you have. You're smart. You're way ahead. You don't complain or blame. You're taking responsibility. Avoid dwelling on what you don't have or you could end up feeling deficient or resentful. Appreciate what you already have while you add and improve your lot.

5 Do something! Choose something that you've been talking about, thinking about for some time, ➤

➤ taking singing lessons, joining Amnesty, changing your job, moving house, whatever. Take responsibility for making it happen. Take the first step today. Demonstrate to yourself that you're a woman or man of action. You wait for no one. You're a doer. You take responsibility. Right attitude. Right action. That's you.

Moral: Treat yourself with dignity and proceed to move toward your fullest expression and highest potential, knowing that *you* are the authority over *you*.

4

Think big

I still get letters from teenagers asking how I did it, and I still enjoy telling them that I did it by not going to journalism school, not getting an education and not training in the provinces as the NUJ always demanded and still advises. Feet first into the legend, that's the only way to go.

JULIE BURCHILL

This is Britain's most controversial journalist, Julie Burchill writing in her autobiography, *I Knew I Was Right*. Don't you just love that brass neck, the guts? Julie Burchill knew she was more than good enough. At 16, when she got her first job on the *NME* (*New Musical Express*) she knew that she knew her stuff. She'd been practising her craft for practically all of those 16 years.

By her own authority, she was ready to go to work. She is both loved and loathed by the British public, but no one could fail to admire the power of her self-belief.

Cut to a recent client of mine. Educated at a US Ivy League college, highly paid career as an investment banker in London, post-graduate journalism course passed with flying colours – now ready for a career change – all by the time she's 25! Not bad going. Except the one asset Jennifer needs more than any other can't be got from another exam, course or qualification – first-class self-belief. Jennifer sees herself as under-qualified. Julie Burchill sees herself as beyond qualifications.

➤ Get gutsy – get ahead

Jennifer's self-belief is feeble. Julie's towering. How's yours? If you had the gutsiness of a Julie Burchill, what would you consider, what would you contemplate that you might not otherwise? Do you play safe – with your own life? Think about it. Do you keep yourself small? Do you stop yourself from thinking big?

A really effective way of keeping small is to aim small. When England captain David Beckham was interviewed after crashing out of the 2002 World Cup after being defeated by Brazil, this is what he said, 'Well, I think we did pretty good. We came here expecting to reach the quarter-finals, whereas Brazil came here to win.' And we know that Brazil did indeed go on to win the 2002 World Cup. England failed to reach the semi-finals. Whilst I fully appreciate that Brazil are a tremendous team, nonetheless Beckham's attitude is disastrous. Aiming to reach the quarter-finals is feeble. How different might they have played had they been playing to win?

➤ Colossal self-belief

Contrast this with the Wimbledon Men's Final the year before on 9th July 2001. No one who saw that match will ever forget it. Goran Ivanisevic, a wild card entry, a no-hoper in theory, took on and beat Australia's Pat Rafter, one of the world's best. No one expected Goran to win and you didn't have to be a tennis expert to see that his game was vastly inferior to many of his opponents, including his semi-final opponent, Tim Henman.

But Goran Ivanisevic had something none of the others had. He had colossal self-belief. What we saw that day was the sort of faith that moves mountains. What Goran did that day went beyond winning a tennis match; he showed us what can be done if we really believe in ourselves.

Maria Sharapova is another Wimbledon name who stunned the crowd with her tennis ability in 2004. At just 17, she powered her way brilliantly to the final and beat Serena Williams to take the title. 'I knew I could achieve many things if I worked hard and if I believed in myself,' said the young Russian, who left her mother and home as a six-year-old to train in America. 'It comes naturally to fight. I've always been a competitor. I've always wanted to play matches and play points. I always wanted to compete – and I wanted to win.'

Evolutionary biologist Dr Dominic Johnson of Harvard University has studied the phenomenon of the winning underdog and believes the reason is due to self-belief, however irrational. 'If you believe you will win then you will win,' he asserts. 'This self-belief has probably evolved by natural selection and started thousands of years ago when we were still primitive hunter gatherers.'

For the great boxer Muhammad Ali, sport was a way of fighting for freedom – his own and his people's. As the young fighter Cassius Clay, he rose to prominence at the time of the civil rights struggle in America and became a cultural hero, redefining what a sports hero could do. Even in the face of oppression, he never lost his sense of grace; sentenced to five years in prison for refusing to be drafted into the army to fight in Vietnam, he shook hands with the three white security guards as he left the courthouse. This not only reflects his greatness but his unshakeable sense of self.

In the same way that Ali transcended his sport, leaders such as Gandhi and Martin Luther King transcended politics, sharing an unshakeable belief which allowed them to achieve what other, more cautious leaders would have believed was impossible.

➤ Play a bigger game

Go beyond what you think you can do. Believe that anything is attainable. Expect the best. Be optimistic. This is the message to take from Goran Ivanisevic and exceptional people the world over. The bigger the challenge, the more you rise to the occasion. In other words, play a bigger game.

Play a game of tennis with a weaker opponent and your game dips to accommodate them. Play with a better player than yourself and your game invariably improves. In any area of life you don't know how good you are until you meet a big enough challenge. The heroes of the Second World War were originally everyday folk who found themselves tested as never before. Thousands of ordinary men and women – not professional soldiers – became extraordinary. Why? Because the situation demanded it. Without that urgency they might never have known how smart, brave, resourceful and downright magnificent they really were.

When, in 2000, over 100 Battle of Britain heroes were reunited, many talked of their fear, but also of how they overcame it. 'I'd be dishonest if I said I was never frightened,' said one Spitfire pilot, Air Commodore Archie Winskill, then in his 80s, 'but I learned to live for the day and never think further ahead than the next battle. I was serving my country and that gave me a huge sense of pride. Fate had produced people such as me to do a job and we did it without question. I was glad I could.'

➤ *Untapped potential*

Who knows what lurks beneath your surface? Do you? Unless you think big enough, you might not. One of the most popular British TV programmes is *Faking It*, where a plucky individual is groomed for four intense weeks to acquire – perfectly – a new skill. You see hot dog sellers turned into prize winning haute cuisine chefs, a sheep shearer turned into a hip London hair stylist, a macho sailor into an outrageous drag artist. One chap began the programme as a painter and decorator. Four weeks later he had morphed into a contemporary artist, his works sharing gallery space with leading young British artists. Some months later the programme makers revisited him. He was getting ready for the opening of his first solo exhibition, in a prestigious gallery in his hometown of Liverpool. It was a spectacular success. He was not a little shocked that people were happy to pay thousands for his efforts. His keenest observation in all of this transformation was simply that without the programme he might never have discovered the genuine talent that he undoubtedly had. Without it he might have carried on painting walls and stripping wallpaper forever.

Another compulsive reality show was *Jamie's Kitchen*, in

which Jamie Oliver took on the task of teaching 15 jobless teenagers how to run a restaurant. The going was tough, and some fell by the wayside, but one of the nine unemployed youngsters to stay the course was Tim Siadatan, whose life has changed forever. A chef at Jamie's not-for-profit restaurant Fifteen, Tim is now planning to open his own chain of diners one day. He says, 'What Jamie has done is amazing; he's taught us that with passion and determination you can get any career you want and be a success, a real heavy duty success. He has given us a passion for a career and has instilled love for it in us. I love going to work, and how many people can say that? We now all believe we can do something with our lives.'

➤ Money doesn't buy happiness

This isn't just a question of money. As many lottery winners have discovered, money doesn't guarantee happiness. In fact, most lottery winners, a year after their windfall, have been found to be usually as happy or as miserable as they were before. But what if you think big? What if you put some of that windfall to good use? If the example of Ray and Barbara Wragg is anything to go by, the results can be awesome.

When the Sheffield couple scooped a £7.6 million jackpot, they decided the best way to enjoy their new-found wealth was to give it away. In less than two years, they gave £6 million to relatives, friends and good causes, saying they were thrilled to have the chance to be able to be so generous. 'You hear lots of people saying winning the lottery has made them miserable – it hasn't done that for us,' said Ray Wragg. Of course they spent some on themselves, swapping their council house for a five-bedroom home and treating themselves to a new car and holidays. But they also gave thousands of pounds to local hospitals, and bought Disney show tickets and chocolates at Christmas and Easter for hundreds of inner-city school children. 'We wrote out a "gift list",' explains Barbara. 'Children, family, then hospitals, charities and friends. Well, we can afford it, can't we? So that's why we did it. When we give away money it's brilliant.'

Anita Roddick made her fortune as founder of The Body Shop, but now talks of her desire to give her wealth away: 'Being generous is a bloody great exit to life.'

While we may not all have lottery numbers to come up, or a Naked Chef to step in and transform our lives, we can all do a stock-take on our hopes and dreams. Think about yourself. Do you think small when it comes to you and your life? Have you shut down, closed off possibilities anywhere, resigned yourself to more 'realistic' ambitions? Are you reluctant to put yourself forward because you are too modest or lack confidence? It's one thing to change your mind about what you want or, on reflection, realise you never really wanted it that much. But giving up without ever trying in the first place may well come back to haunt you. Thankfully you're smart enough to avoid that fate.

THE WORK

1 Think bigger! Understand the principle of rising to the occasion. You'll simply play a bigger game. You fancy taking up jogging? Enrol for a 5km race and watch yourself get ready.

2 Be optimistic. You're no wimp. Never talk like one. Never, ever say, I can't, it's impossible. Aim to achieve. Intend to succeed. Believe that anything is attainable. Do not for one moment think that you can't achieve your goal.

3 Plan to win. Get a strategy in place. Think about every step along the path to achieving that goal. Don't be vague. Get it on paper. Be organised.

4 Get committed. The moment you really commit is when things start to happen. As Goethe said a century and a half ago, 'The moment one commits oneself then providence moves too. All sorts of things occur to help one that would never have otherwise occurred. A whole new stream of events, all manner of unforeseen incidents and chance meetings, and material assistance come forth which no one could have dreamt would appear.'

5 Get excited. Why bother extending yourself if there's no good reason? Create some urgency about your goal so you feel sufficiently compelled to dig a little deeper. Choose one thing this week that involves you biting off more than you think you can chew. If it's important enough, you'll handle it.

Moral: Impossible is an opinion.

5

Recover faster

Character cannot be developed in ease and quiet. Only through experiences of trial and suffering can the soul be strengthened, vision cleared, ambition inspired and success achieved.

HELEN KELLER

We've already covered a lot of ground. Day by day your overall belief in yourself has been growing. You know the vital importance of nurturing it, making yourself strong and healthy. You can recognise those who have it and those who don't. You may also have come across people who had it but lost it. It happens.

How does a person lose faith in themselves? Why would

someone stop believing in themselves? Can you really have self-belief one year and not the next? Absolutely. Ask one of the long-term unemployed. Ask a teenager who's sleeping rough. Ask a man or woman whose business went bankrupt. Ask someone who hasn't dated for a few years, after a big rejection. Building self-belief is one thing. Keeping it – something else altogether.

But even something as potentially devastating as bankruptcy can give you a chance for a new start. When, due to what she calls 'a mixture of stupidity and bad luck', the television presenter Clarissa Dickson Wright (she of *Two Fat Ladies* fame) declared herself bankrupt for the second time in 2003, she said the experience helped her draw a line under the past. 'I am a believer in bankruptcy. It draws a line under a series of mishaps or disasters and leaves one free to sort things out with the help of an expert, and move on.'

➤ *Don't let setbacks stop you*

In business, those at the top of their game know that to be a success, you can't let setbacks stop you in your tracks. The retail tycoon Philip Green is just one example of how to recover faster. The billionaire entre-preneur left school at 15 with no qualifications but has made his fortune by breathing new life into ailing busi-nesses, first Bhs, and then the clothing group Arcadia (who own Top Shop, Miss Selfridge and Wallis). With his talent for understanding what mass-market cus-tomers want, he's been called 'the original brash market trader', but has made himself the most powerful man on the high street. A classic success story, you might think, but his business ventures have not always been such a success. His first dealings saw one company go bust, and another two go under with thousands of pounds' worth of debts.

On the other side of the Atlantic, Donald Trump is one of America's most high profile and successful property developers, and the star of *The Apprentice*, the smash-hit US reality series. His business career has seen more highs and more lows than most but what drove him on after the 1990 property crash in which he lost millions was his philosophy that you never give up. 'I'm not a quitter,' he says. 'So I just kept going and came back. My two most important rules on how to become suc-cessful are that you have to enjoy what you're doing, because if you don't you'll never be successful. And number two is that you can never give up or quit. If there is a concrete wall ahead of you, you have to go through it. I know many people who are brilliant but they're not successful. I know others who are not nearly as smart, but they are great success stories because they never give up.'

The dotcom fever in the 1990s was a classic example of how success and failure can be inextricably linked. At one point, the computer boom was creating 64 millionaires every day, many of them based in California's Silicon Valley. The inevitable crash saw their new-found riches evaporate, and for some, the fallout was devastating. They were the ones who'd made it personal, who built their self-esteem on their new fortunes. The more they identified with their wealth, the more the change had a severe psychological impact on them.

But interestingly, most of the young internet entrepreneurs refused to allow failure to define their lives. To get to the top in the first place, they needed unshakeable self-belief, and this remained intact, regardless of their bank balance. For them, the future was what mattered, the next big idea, the next money making scheme. Some even put their experiences to use by giving speeches about them at other company conferences!

Now an important lesson has been learned. Failure is looked on as something to learn from and apply in future businesses, and, if a firm isn't viable, it's closed down quickly and the people regroup and start again.

➤ *Life tests you*

Holding on to your self-belief is easy when things are going well. It's when the going gets tough that you have to watch out. Handling yourself well in turmoil is vital if you are to live an interesting life. Life will definitely take it out of you. Every one of us will have our fair share of testing, defeats, disappointments, criticism and even condemnation. No one gets a totally easy life. The question is – how do you handle it?

First, realise that failure need not be the end of your dreams. Never see failure as a defeat or something that marks you permanently. Instead, develop what psychologists call a 'rebound personality'. Rebound personalities are renewed, even inspired, by failure.

You're much better placed to handle challenges if you're already operating from a strong foundation of self-belief. Without that solid bedrock underpinning you, challenges will knock you harder than they should. You'll be thrown off course too easily, undermined at the first hurdle. All the attention that you've been paying to your foundations over the past few weeks has been invaluable, but what about a really big knock? What do you do when your very foundation is shaken?

You need to know how to put yourself back together again. You need to be able to dig deeper into yourself to emerge stronger, clearer and better than ever. Understand: a crisis will never leave you where it finds you. You'll be weakened or strengthened by it. It's entirely down to you. It's not what happens that poses the greatest threat – it's your interpretation of it. Remember, your greatest ally or most powerful enemy is one and the same person – you.

There's no one better positioned than you to do maximum damage to yourself. When life is at its toughest, you can turn the gun on yourself – often called shooting yourself in the foot! Or you can rise up to your full powers, get into the right frame of mind and resolve not to be beaten, least of all by yourself. Whether you acknowledge it or not, a crisis always hands you this choice.

➤ *Life's survivors*

Liza Minnelli was never going to have a humdrum life. As a baby, her first visitor was Frank Sinatra, while her mother Judy Garland battled her own demons until dying when Liza was 23. Not only has Liza had more highs and lows than most, they've all been played out in public. An Oscar in her 20s for her brilliant portrayal of Sally Bowles in *Cabaret*, packed out concert halls, drug abuse ... they were all well documented, but fans were shocked when she appeared grossly overweight in a wheelchair. But within a year, she'd lost an incredible six stone, and had bounced back in irrepressible style, marrying flamboyant producer David Gest in an OTT showbiz ceremony. No one was particularly surprised when the marriage soon hit the rocks, but after a journalist commented she'd had a lot of problems, she replied, 'Haven't you?' The point is everyone has problems; it's how we deal with them that counts.

The glossy magazine world is notoriously competitive, but one woman who carved her way to the very top is Mandi Norwood. This famously ambitious journalist fulfilled her dream of editing her own title by the time she was 25, eventually becoming editor-in-chief of *Cosmopolitan* for five years until moving to New York to take on the job of turning around the ailing *Mademoiselle* magazine. When sales failed to pick up, owners Conde Nast folded the magazine and Mandi was left out of a job for the first time in nearly 20 years. She could've slunk back home with her tail between her legs, but that's not her style. Instead, she stayed put, and bounced back in style, writing the best-selling book *Sex and the Married Woman*, inspired by the confessions of her married girlfriends. Her failure to make a success of *Mademoiselle* left the high profile media star open to sniping, but she didn't let that dim her ambition. 'Yes, I am ambitious,' she says, 'but I'm surprised it's worthy of note. I'm from Thatcher's generation – ambition was bred into you.'

Mandi says she never ever considered returning to London. 'That's not how I operate. I like to take control of my own destiny. I don't like circumstance driving the pattern of my life. I didn't want to feel defeated. My mother always said: "Don't let anybody tell you that you can't do this or that." You get an opportunity, you grit your teeth and, who knows, it might come off.'

➤ *Overcoming tragedy*

When the Labour Chancellor of the Exchequer Gordon Brown and his wife lost their first-born baby at just 10 days old, he said the tragedy served to remind him and his wife Sarah of the importance of using his time to make a difference. 'Jennifer's death has made us more determined to do things that are right,' he said. 'Jennifer is an inspiration to us. We have thought about what is important, and you have to use your time.'

➤ *Let go of fear*

In their book, *Life Lessons: How Our Mortality Can Teach Us About Life And Living*, authors Elisabeth Kubler-Ross and David Kessler talk about the lessons they learnt through their work with the dying and those who have survived life-threatening illnesses.

And the most important lesson from those that have looked death in the eye? To let go of fear. 'So much is possible when fear no longer holds us captive. To transcend fear, we have to practise. If you tackle your secret passions, you will not face regrets of a life half lived. We all have our dreams. But, sadly, we are also filled with reasons why we shouldn't fulfil them. Life is over sooner than we think.'

➤ Authenticity

Deep inside us, there is someone we were meant to be. But, too often, we define ourselves by our circumstances and feel great only if things are going well. If life goes badly, we feel worthless or look to other things or people such as loved ones or the 'perfect' job, to define us and prop up our self-esteem. We take on certain roles because they are lucrative yet once we achieve them we feel empty. We discover our true identities by finding out what we want – and do not want – to do. This means we have a right to acknowledge what we enjoy, right down to our job and the clothes we wear, and not allow ourselves to do something because someone thinks it's our role.

Nigella Lawson, the seductive chef whose best-selling books and TV series have made her one of the most famous women in Britain, credits her late husband John Diamond with much of her success by boosting her self-confidence. He constantly told her, 'you can, you can, you can,' recalls her sister Horatia. 'John was an optimist,' concurs Nigella. 'The world was his reward.' So when he was struck dumb by cancer of the neck and tongue, the most important voice in her life was silenced. 'That's how I began talking more. Just because I had to talk for him, because no one could understand him.' John Diamond died in 2001, just as Nigella's career was taking off.

Laurie Anderson, the influential American musician and performance artist is in her 50s now, but still remembers vividly the time when she was a child of seven and taking care of her three-year-old twin brothers when they fell into a frozen lake. With no adults around, Laurie dived into the icy water to rescue them, put one under each arm, and raced home, saving both their lives. The accident could so easily have had tragic consequences, and she worried that she might be blamed for putting her brothers in danger. But her family simply praised her for her quick thinking. 'That episode was the first time I saw how a terrible failure could be a kind of success, and that maybe they weren't so far away from each other.'

➤ *Overcoming disaster*

In 1999, the Scottish mountaineer, Jamie Andrew, lost both his hands and feet to frostbite after being trapped by a freak storm in the French Alps for five days and nights. The 28-year-old watched, helpless, as his best friend Jamie Fisher died beside him. Lying in hospital, being spoonfed by nurses, he could have let this terrible ordeal destroy his life, but Jamie's indomitable spirit won through. 'After what happened, I quickly realised that everything my life had been built on before was now invalid, except for my relationships with my friends and family,' he wrote. 'All my hopes and dreams and intentions, every plan I had ever made, was written off. But you've got to fill your head with new plans, new dreams. Even in hospital I started planning first of all that I would learn to feed myself. That I would be able to get out of bed, to walk, to take care of myself, to go back home and live with my girlfriend Anna again. Dreams that were every bit as challenging and fulfilling as my ambitions were before.'

Failure was never an option and Jamie astonished doctors with his determination and, staying true to his vow that he would climb again, within a year he had achieved the unthinkable and climbed Ben Nevis on his new artificial legs. Five years later he has taken up mountaineering and rock climbing again, as well as skiing, and even completed the London Marathon. He married Anna, and now has had a baby daughter, Iris. 'I don't like to be held back by things,' he says.

When the going gets tough, you need to think fast, regroup and recover. You need a strategy, a back-up plan. This is it.

➤ *Recover faster*

1 Wake up. However unpleasant or gruesome, grasp the problem. Avoiding it, burying it always makes it worse. Don't let things fester. Front up. Admit what's really going on. The energy that you're using to resist the issue could be far better employed handling it.

2 Don't undermine yourself. If you've made mistakes, seriously got things wrong, get the lesson – fast. Otherwise you'll repeat it until you do. Get it and then get over it. Your entire focus and attention needs to be focused outwards, not inwards, action orientated, not spent picking at yourself. At a time like this you could do colossal damage to yourself that could be exceedingly difficult and time consuming to repair later. If you catch yourself beginning to inflict damage, stop it immediately.

3 Refuse to be beaten. Defeat is not an option, whatever the outcome. Your handling of the crisis allows you to feel victorious. Knowing that you rose to the occasion, did everything you could, applied every ounce of ingenuity and resourcefulness that you could muster, and then some, lets you look yourself in the eye.

4 Embrace failure. You must fail in order to succeed. Fear of failure is the real demon. Look at any powerful man or woman who has achieved success and you'll find failure. It's the risk one takes, the price you sometimes pay for an ambitious life. Above all, don't take failure personally. You are not a failure.

However badly things have gone, get this – failure is not the worst thing ever, never trying in the first place is.

5 Watch your interpretation. When all's said and done, check yourself over. Is there any internal bleeding, any oozing wounds that could destroy, or seriously delay a full recovery? Give yourself a thorough once-over. Be very, very careful to clear up and thoroughly deal with anything that might linger, fester and poison. Ensure that you're able to return to your life and build a future for yourself with all your faculties entirely restored and intact. Otherwise, you run the risk of joining the ranks of the walking wounded – those who were tested and shrank, or those who found their efforts wanting. Winston Churchill himself said this, 'A successful person is somebody who goes from one failure to another without any loss of enthusiasm.' Make sure that's you.

THE WORK

1 Speed up your recovery. Even on everyday things, pay attention and handle upsets quickly. As soon as you notice you're making heavy weather of something, stop. Resolve the matter satisfactorily and move on.

2 Run a check. Scan yourself to spot any lingering limitations, ongoing slights that you may be carrying within yourself. By all means, make connections between then and now, the event, circumstances that you have used to undermine you.

3 Let it go. You may well have acted less than brilliantly, on reflection. Grasp this and all the stark lessons. Then, let it go. Make your peace – with yourself. Otherwise, you're set on course to undermine yourself from here on in.

4 Handle criticism. Sometimes other people have a point. If you feel you need to make amends, do so. By all means, delve into yourself with interesting questions. But, do move on. Seal yourself up. Don't

allow your power to gush out of you in recrimination. Constant picking and haemorrhaging is not healthy for anyone.

5 Don't dumb down. Check whether you've resigned yourself to smaller aspirations, more modest ambitions, based on your experience, or your interpretation of those experiences. Dust yourself down. Wash off that experience and get ready to move on.

Moral: The future belongs to those who believe in the possibility of their dreams.

6

You're fabulous!

Live all you can; it's a mistake not to. It doesn't so much matter what you do in particular, so long as you have had your life. If you haven't had that, what have you had?

HENRY JAMES, *The Ambassadors*

Right from the outset I've been coaching you, coaxing you, challenging you to upgrade your opinion of yourself. Building and maintaining powerful self-belief is a choice. It isn't something you must be born with. It doesn't matter how low your levels have been – you can upgrade any time you like. Remember in the very first chapter I asked you to identify your current levels of self-belief? Now I want you to notice how you've progressed. More importantly, it's time to look at what you're going to do with your new power!

How did a lack of self-belief hold you back before? What difference did you imagine, hope for when we started out? Now is the time to get absolutely clear what an upscaled life looks like with you running on full power. What does a revved-up, pumped-up you look like? You know how to turn it on, take responsibility, conquer your fear of failure, fake it when necessary and recover fast. With all that know-how, you're way ahead! The fears and self-doubt that hold the average person back have little power over you. You have far greater self-knowledge and self-control than most people. You know how to handle yourself. It's called self-management.

➤ *Real power*

In squaring up to yourself, you've achieved a level of internal power that a great many people do not possess. Your self-assurance has grown. I bet you like yourself more. You have ambitions for yourself, for your life. Feeling powerful and enthusiastic about yourself lets you entertain those ambitions more enthusiastically – and seriously. Take pen and paper and briefly note down your responses to these questions:

1 How could my life change with the self-belief to do, say or try anything?

2 What are the most important things I want to do now that I have much greater self-belief?

3 How have I changed in the way I see myself ?

4 What do I want to achieve now that fear of failure doesn't stop me from taking risks?

5 What would I do if I pushed myself beyond the limits of my comfort zone?

These are fascinating questions for you right now. You need spend only a few minutes here to get your imagination going. What I'm encouraging you to see is an exciting vision for your life. Possessing strong self-belief is a fabulous feeling in itself but the real advantage of it is that it opens life up for you. You see possibilities and opportunities where you didn't before. It's the same world. You're just looking at it differently. It's you that's changed. So, in essence, what would a fabulous life look like for you? The very act of committing this picture to paper is vital.

It's you raising your expectations and taking them seriously.

➤ *Demand more*

This new self-belief has advantages at work and at home. Use it to ensure you never undersell yourself. It's your powerful tool to get the best possible life for yourself. Use it at work to ensure you are getting the deal you deserve. Women in particular often fail to get what they really want because they lack the negotiating skills to succeed. Research carried out by Linda Babcock, Professor of Economics at Carnegie Mellon University in Pennsylvania found that in all types of situation – from asking for job promotion to getting their men to help around the home, women started negotiations less often and demanded much less than men. And when they did speak up, they were also far less successful. On average, women negotiated pay rises that were 30% lower than men. Babcock argues that women are too unassertive to take the lead in making decisions or standing up for themselves.

Another startling study of 24 blue chip companies

showed that less than five per cent of senior managers were women. Some might blame that on the glass ceiling, but psychologists who analysed the findings declared that ambitious women were failing to make it to the top because they waste time trying to be nice. Women thought they must be attractive, sociable and deferent to their seniors to be promoted, whereas in fact bosses just wanted to know whether candidates could get the job done. The desire to please was getting the women nowhere.

➤ *Raising difficult subjects*

This reluctance to raise awkward issues can leave you trapped and frustrated. A recent study into UK employees revealed that one in 10 would rather leave their job than broach a difficult subject with their bosses. Those 'difficult subjects'? Top of the list were asking for a salary rise or promotion. Again, it's women in particular who are the ones losing out. Nearly 60 per cent admit to holding back from talking to their boss about promotion and pay rises out of fear.

Winning promotion and getting a pay rise all comes

down to how much confidence you have. This isn't about arrogance – it's about the kind of confidence that comes with high self-esteem, saying you value yourself and being direct.

➤ *Aspire more*

Remember: what you think, you create. First comes your thought about yourself, then follows the outer world of physical manifestation. Perspective – thought – reality. If you don't think something is possible you won't take even the first step towards creating it. If your self-belief is shaky, then you'll falter at the first setback, confirming your strongest beliefs about yourself.

One woman who has aspired more is Catherine Zeta-Jones. Her determination to succeed has taken her from a Welsh council estate to movie star A-list. As one of the stars of *The Darling Buds of May,* she could have settled for a limited television career in Britain, but instead chose to move to Hollywood where she rein-vented herself in spectacular fashion. How spectacular? Well, the actress recently signed a nine film deal worth £54 million. But this fabulous career didn't drop into her lap. As she points out, 'It takes a lot more than just being pretty. I came to America to join the lines of beautiful, talented, creative people who all flock to the nucleus of the business to do exactly what I wanted to do. It was very difficult at the beginning and I was very apprehensive about the whole thing. But I persevered because I never wanted to look back in years ahead and think, "if only I'd had the guts to give it a shot".'

Holding the highest ideas for yourself is the glorious challenge I'm throwing you. I invite you to sketch out the grandest version of yourself and your life that you can possibly imagine. Shortly, we'll look at you taking action. Just now, raise those expectations of you. Why not? If not you, then who?

In working with many, many clients over the years I never cease to be amazed at how entirely consistent people's aspirations are with their talents. Whether they want a complete change in their life or simply want to move up in what they're already doing, I can't remember a single instance that didn't 'fit'. In all instances the big leap forwards came from them believing in that 'fit' – that they were intrinsically equipped to have, be or do the very thing they wanted. In some cases they needed to get a few practical skills notched up, but that's straight-forward enough. The critical point is to see the rightness of what you're aspiring to and the person you are.

➤ You're the talent

Let me give you a few examples. If someone expresses an ambition to be a fiction writer, I'll ask them to explain, to justify why they think they should be doing that. I probe into their childhood to look for the evidence that points to their innate talents and desires. They'll tell me of the writing competitions they used to win, year after year, the books they read while friends were out playing or dating, the short stories they've got tucked away. This is the sort of evidence I'm looking for. I then highlight the significance of this for them, so they appreciate the rightness of their dream. The more they pay attention to this personal history, the more they believe in their talent, in their power, in themselves. Who are they not to write? And if not them, then who? And if not now, when? I remember joking with one new self-doubting client – now a successful novelist – that at 37, she had over 30 years writing experience behind her – and so she had.

Another client, Sarah wanted a change of career. She loved the idea of being her own boss, having her own business, but in what area? She said there was nothing obvious that she was really good at or loved to do. I asked her to describe her home for me, what would stand out for me as I looked around. Without hesitation, she answered, 'cookery books, everywhere, first editions, Mrs Beeton, Nigella Lawson, cake recipes handed down from my grandmother, they're everywhere.' I paused. She heard what she'd just said. Aha.

From that moment onwards we got busy working on the plan to fit a business to her passion. Shortly, she'll open the most fabulous, glamorous food shop in London, probably the first of many. Whilst many of our sessions concentrated on the logistics and practicalities of her plan, I frequently bolstered her belief in the exquisite fit between her self and her plan. The more she saw her business as the unfolding of her intrinsic talent and life-long passion, the more ardently she believed in herself and her success. Pure destiny, freewill and personal responsibility blending together.

Was she 'qualified' as an expert foodie? Of course she

was. By her own authority. In her own eyes – first and foremost – most importantly.

Rose Gray is the co-founder of one of London's best known and successful restaurants, the River Café. But this was no overnight success story. Rose met her friend and partner Ruth Rogers when they were both working as graphic designers in 1970; they shared a love of food and dreamed of starting their own restaurant. It wasn't until more than 16 years later that the pair finally opened the River Café. Rose says now of this decade and a half wait, 'as chefs we were completely untrained, but after a while you think, I love food, I love cooking, and that's really how I want to earn my living. But we lacked courage. Looking back, we definitely should have done it sooner, instead of slogging it out as graphic designers for so many years.'

As I write this, I hear the news that the great psychologist Elizabeth Kubler-Ross has just died. I am instantly reminded of something she wrote that seems so relevant to our conversation here today: 'after your death, when most of you for the first time realise what life here is all about, you will begin to see that your life here is almost nothing but the sum total of every choice you have made during every moment of your life. Your thoughts, which you are responsible for, are as real as your deeds. You will begin to realise that every word and every deed affects your life and has also touched thousands of lives.'

➤ Do the right thing

Someone who has combined all his passions to create the life he loves is the gardener and TV presenter Alan Titchmarsh. 'People say, "oh, you're so lucky!" I really know I am, but I've taken risks. Years ago, I threw in my job when I had a wife and a baby on the way. Most people said I was mad, but I had to do it. I'm very much driven by heart and tempered by head. Always, always, always listen to that inner voice. Whenever you don't, it generally doesn't work.'

Alan also believes in doing the right thing. 'It's important to do good. To leave here a better place when you shuffle off at the end.'

He's so right, and studies seem to bear this out. One study found that older people who are helpful to others are 60 per cent more likely to outlive those who are miserable and self-centred. 'Making a contribution to the lives of other people may help to extend our lives,' says the paper's author, psychologist Stephanie Brown. The study of nearly 1,000 people concluded that it isn't what we get from relationships that makes contact with others so beneficial. It's what we give.

Pyschology professor Martin Seligman has made the study of happiness his life's work. In his book, *Authentic Happiness*, he identifies three types of happiness: the pleasant life, the good life, and the meaningful life. Here's what he has to say about each one: 'The pleasant life is the Hollywood version of happiness, which is about maximising the pleasures and minimising the pains.' (Think shopping, drug taking and casual sex.) The good life, focused on work, love, play and parenting, is traditionally the one we aspire to and more rewarding. But Dr Seligman says for true satisfaction, this has to come with a meaningful life, which he defines as 'serving the cause of something bigger than yourself'. This is crucial because, 'We all need meaning in our lives. Without it, we are just fidgeting until we die.'

➤ *Let go of anger*

The Hollywood actress Susan Sarandon looks fabulous in her 50s, something she puts down to her state of mind as well as her Pilates passion. 'Letting go of anger and hate is the key to staying young,' she says. 'Hatred is definitely unsexy and not great for your skin.'

➤ *Downshifting*

The trend towards downshifting after years of slogging it out in the rat race is well documented, but interestingly, a new breed of young, previously high achieving drop-outs are making the decision to quit the corporate grind before they've even hit 30. They're not prepared to endure years of disillusionment – they want personal fulfilment from the outset, even if it means turning their backs on the chance to earn enough money to help set them up for life. In the same way that it's never too late to make that change, it's also never too early!

➤ *What do you need to notice about you?*

What are you missing and missing out on? It's all in the details of your life. What are the clues you've glossed over? What's important for you to notice? What evidence do you need to accumulate? What do you need to believe about yourself?

This isn't fiction. I don't want fabrication. I'm after hard facts, times and dates, conversations, compelling proof. Keep this line of enquiry open. In a notebook, write this heading, 'What I need to believe about me'. Get clear on the precise nature of your investigation. Then set about building a watertight case, rock solid, irrefutable evidence that proves conclusively – to you – what you need to truly, deeply believe about you. Then, believing in yourself is easy. You refer back to the evidence to reinforce yourself as and when you need to.

THE WORK

1 How much have you upgraded yourself? Keep on moving up. Don't stop here. Take you and your progress out to lunch. Dine on your developments. Drink a toast to you. Self-praise is vital praise!

2 What's your hesitation? Check that you don't have a lurking fear of being more powerful. Remind yourself that healthy self-belief is silent. It doesn't scream for attention, beg for approval, shout to be noticed. That's reserved for the most needy in our society. Not you.

3 Live well. Live the life of an ISBer. You have all the knowledge you need. You're fully equipped. Now, live the dream. Take a few risks. Step out – your belief in yourself doesn't depend on constant and never-ending success.

4 What's your purpose? Ensure your personal power is aligned to the bigger picture. What contribution does a pumped-up, fully-realised you make to the world? Enshrine your life and power with a higher ➤

➤ significance. As the very fabulous Susan Sarandon says: 'It's everyone's responsibility to be the protagonist in their own life and ask questions. When something doesn't feel right in your heart, you should try to find some way to do something about it.'

5 You're fabulous! Here you are, taking full responsibility for making your time here on earth work, for your own good and the good of all. You're not moaning. You're not blaming. You're just getting on with making it all work, doing your best and being your best. How downright fabulous is that? It's terrific. You're terrific. Keep that firmly in mind, especially when you really need to.

Moral: The absence of courage causes more suffering than can ever be calculated.

7

Building a successful identity

It is not because things are difficult we do not dare; it is because we do not dare that they are difficult.

SENECA

➤ *Perseverance*

Tina Brown is the shrewd networker and talented British editor who went to New York and rose to the top of her profession when she rescued two ailing magazines, *Vanity Fair* and the *New Yorker*. With her husband, the ex-*Sunday Times* editor Harold Evans, they became Manhattan's most powerful media couple. Craving a new challenge she launched *Talk* in 1999, an upmarket celebrity and gossip magazine. It closed after two and a half years, but Brown remained unapologetic. 'There is nothing more boring than the undefeated. Any great, long career has at least one flame-out in it.'

➤ *Failure makes you try harder*

Beyonce Knowles is one of the most successful R&B singers in recent years. She's not only topped the charts both sides of the Atlantic with 30 million albums sold to date, but is carving a successful movie career for herself too. Both are hugely competitive industries – to rise to the top in both takes not just talent but a complete belief in yourself. Much credit for this can go towards the attitudes fostered in Beyonce by her father Mathew Knowles. He's the career strategist who has spearheaded her success and instilled in her the belief that failure should never be something to be feared. He learnt an early lesson when the fledgling Destiny's Child (then known as Girls Time) lost in a TV talent show. Afterwards, the show's producer told Knowles that 'it was the ones who lose who often go onto win. Because they re-dedicated.' Now Knowles says, 'to be successful in life, there has to be failure.'

➤ Losing money

Record producer Pete Waterman helped launch Kylie on the road to pop superstardom, and was a judge on *Pop Idol*. He's seen both success and failure, but says, 'I learn by making mistakes. In the early 1990s the public perception was that I was earning £1 million a day – the truth was that I was spending £1.2 million a day. You don't know that until someone says, "you owe us £9.5 million". I crawled back with my loyal staff, by working hard, and paying a fortune to the best financial advisors.'

➤ Comeback kids

The showbusiness world is full of survivors, of come-back kids who refuse to give up or give in. In the early 90s, Kylie Minogue's musical career had stalled. An ex-*Neighbours* star who'd had a few hits, she wasn't taken seriously as a singer and was in danger of fading off the public radar once and for all. One radio station even ran an advertising campaign that announced: 'We've done something to improve Kylie's records. We've banned them!' Undeterred, she kick-started her faltering career by taking a leaf out of Madonna's book and learning the power of reinvention. Through sheer determination, and by surrounding herself with the right people – crucially the best songwriters and stylists in the business – she re-emerged as the glossiest, sexiest chart topper of the millennium.

In the UK, there can sometimes be a mean-spirited culture of gloating over failure. Never more so than by the press in the case of high profile, successful Brits when failure is something to be vicariously enjoyed.

A young Briton who refused to give in is Kelly Brook. She was the former glamour model who was given her showbusiness break when she took over co-presenting *The Big Breakfast* with Johnny Vaughn. Inexperienced and nervous, she was mocked by critics, and ended up being dumped by her employers after just six months. But she had the last laugh by taking herself to Los Angeles where she reinvented herself as an in-demand actress, impressing producers and gaining movie roles. When invited to take part in a documentary about the history of the early morning show, she didn't waste words, but sent a fax which said simply: 'Kelly gone to Hollywood'. She has said of her public failure on live TV, 'something like that either makes you or breaks you. It gave me the motivation to prove myself and now I have moved on and done even better.'

➤ Facing up to tragedy

For some, it is a random tragedy which brings them face to face with their own mortality.

For Michael J Fox, the moment came at the height of his success. Just 30, the star of the *Back to the Future* trilogy, learned that he had Parkinson's disease, a debilitating condition that normally strikes sufferers in their 50s or 60s. Many would rail at the unfairness of this, but the actor says it opened up a whole new world to him, 'Parkinson's gave me a whole different appreciation for life. I was enriched by how it made me look at things and what it wouldn't let me take for granted any more. It exposed me to new people and new experiences

– you don't get to see those things if you're just skating through life.'

Simon Weston has faced more challenges than most. A handsome young soldier, he was terribly burned by a bomb in the Falklands War and spent four years undergoing the painful skin grafts which cover 80% of his body. His experience would be enough to test the spirit of anyone, and he could so easily have gone under and wallowed in depression. Instead, he found meaning to his life by helping others, forming Weston Spirit to help motivate inner-city youngsters who feel they have no future. His personal life has turned around too – he has done a parachute jump, run the New York marathon, and is married with three children. 'The most important thing if you do become injured,' says Simon, 'is how you cope. If you spend your life full of bitterness, then you've failed.'

This is borne out by the work with the terminally ill done by Elisabeth Kubler-Ross and David Kessler. They found happiness is a state of mind. To be truly happy, you must live for the moment instead of looking for happiness to come as a reaction to an event in the future. 'We must not give into feelings of victimisation, thinking that everything bad happens to us. Life has loss, recovery, sunshine and rain. It's not personally against us,' they say. 'When we feel good about ourselves, we have more to give.'

➤ Don't let negative comments put you off

Just because something hasn't been done before, doesn't mean it can't be done. JK Rowling was a single mother living on £70 a week benefits when she created Harry Potter while scribbling away in local cafés. What is perhaps not so well known is that she sold her first manuscript for just £1,500. After lunch with the head of the company's children's book division, he told her, 'You'll never make any money out of children's books, Jo.' Eight years later, she is Britain's highest earning woman with a personal fortune of over £200 million.

Kristin Scott Thomas is one of Britain's most successful actresses. But her burning ambition was almost extinguished by a drama teacher who told her that if she wanted to play Lady Macbeth she would have to join a local amateur dramatic company. How small-minded!

Her brilliant career is testament to the fact that thinking small is never the answer. Instead, she moved to France, enrolled in a local drama class and was soon appearing in ever more high profile films.

One defining moment for her was being flown out to meet a casting director early on in her career, who refused to look up when she walked in, talking on the phone while she flicked through Scott Thomas' book. Then, when she had finished, rudely announced she 'could go now'. Kristin is now grateful. 'The great thing about that was that it made me realise I don't need to navigate through all this bullshit. I don't need to let other people treat me like a worm. There are other ways to do it.'

Handling criticism is something that will test your foundation of self-belief and can shake you to your very core. Having a clear and strong foundation of clearly defined self-belief underpinning you will help enormously, but you can still be rocked and unseated by others' attempts to undermine you. When this happens, take time out to examine the claims and if there is genuine fault on your part, face up to this and make amends. If you've made a mess, be big enough and self-assured enough to admit it and clean it up. If you feel you don't have a case to answer and are being unfairly attacked, defend yourself. Reaffirm who you are and shore up your self-belief so you emerge stronger than before. Think of what happens when a healthy immune system has to respond to an outside threat such as germs and how through galvinising its resources it fights off the attack and emerges not weakened but more robust than before. This is exactly how you must be. And the more successful, powerful, ambitious or visible you are, the more prone to criticism you will become. Be ready and be prepared to handle what may come your way.

I had my first taste of this a few years ago when a journalist wrote a personal attack on me and my work in a national newspaper. I was utterly unprepared and caught off-guard by her vitriol and for a very short time it threw me into questioning who I was and the value of the work that I do. The shock of her attack actually weakened me at the knees and I had to grab the nearest chair to hold on to. I reasserted the value and importance of the work I do by reminding myself of my satisfied clients and the thousands of letters and emails I had received over the years from readers of my books. I looked at her situation and career and reminded myself that she was far from totally happy and satisfied with her position and I also realised that she may well have been directed to write a 'critical' piece in the first place. I determined not to allow her poison to infect my picture of myself or my self-belief. So, forewarned is forearmed. Be prepared for criticism and handle it thoroughly when it comes. Guard against any long-term damage to your self-worth and faith in yourself. Draw a line under it as soon as possible and refuse to allow it to follow you around or throw you off course. Sometimes people come to me who have become so weakened by criticism that they've lost their shine and have allowed themselves to be tarnished and their spirit dulled by the mud slinging. I joke that I wish I could put them under a shower to wash all the dirt off!

Ask yourself right now if you're walking around diminished by something someone has thrown at you. Have you taken on someone's comments, begun to believe them and now you dig at yourself? Remember, there is no more powerful loathing as self-loathing. If you're taking swipes at yourself, you'll be far more effective in your undermining than any outsider. Clear up any ambiguity or messes from the past that have left their mark and move on.

Your opinion of yourself is the one that really counts. In time, you will have to answer to *you* for everything you have ever done. Ensure you are able to hold yourself in the highest regard by maintaining your values and principles and continually striving for your own highest standards. Forgiveness is a vital part of any successful long-term relationship so extend it to yourself as you would to another.

➤ *Fear of failure*

Are there certain attributes successful people share? The fascinating BBC documentary *Mind of a Millionaire* suggested that some psychological traits are crucial to how entrepreneurs respond to challenges. Dr Adrian Atkinson, the psychologist studying the behaviour of self-made millionaires during the experiment, pinpointed entrepreneurs' high self-belief. 'They don't recognise failure, and have selective memory when it comes to failure.' The result, he says, is that failures are 're-patterned' as learning curves: while most of us give up, the entrepreneur just keeps on trying. This determination to succeed is all important – the average entrepreneur will have five failed ventures before their first success.

Stephen Palmer, Professor of Psychology at London's City University makes an important point: 'People who turn failure into success blame what they have *done*, not themselves. They see the failure as the result of mistakes they have made, that are not central to their personality. They often see failure as a life event outside their control. If you label yourself as "a failure", it's very difficult to pull yourself out of whatever pit you are in.'

Making failure personal will also make it difficult to be dynamic and decisive in admitting something's not working, cut your losses and run. I've seen people hang on to relationships and businesses long after they should have admitted defeat or shut up shop. I've watched people lose thousands and amass enormous debt, refusing to change direction because it would mean owning up to having got something wrong at the outset. I assure you I have initiated heaps of bright ideas that haven't worked out, and just as many that have. And because I attach no shame in saying something isn't working and shelving it, including handing money back to customers, my vision isn't blurred by my ego's need to be right about everything. And sometimes your ideas are ahead of time or you haven't got your marketing or location right, but whatever the truth, it's vital to address it so that you can get it right next time. Don't let failure or the fear of it hold you hostage in your own life. Break free from this way of thinking and you'll be a lot lighter on your feet as a result.

➤ *Charisma*

How can you develop that indefinable quality which makes one person stand out from the crowd? It's not only about looks. Michael Owen is acknowledged as one of the most talented men ever to don an England football shirt – but charismatic? Hardly. Likewise Gywneth Paltrow – an undeniably beautiful and talented actress, but it's difficult to imagine her lighting up a room in the same way as, say, the glowing Halle Berry, or the vibrant Sharon Stone. The point is that possessing charisma is not just something some lucky people are born with – it's something we can all develop if we have strength of will. Key requirements are a big heart, a genuine interest in others (and no expectation that they are purely there to entertain you), and the ability to put people at ease. From a rather dull teenage Sloane to glittering media icon, Princess Diana developed it. Her metamorphosis was dictated by circumstances. By virtue of his birth, Charles has never had the need for charisma, and thus is never likely to develop it.

➤ *Choose wisely*

The horror writer Stephen King has sold more than 300 million books and is one of the most popular authors in the world. He credits his long-lasting marriage to wife Tabitha and three children as the bedrock of this success. She was the one who pulled him back from the brink of alcoholism and drug abuse in the early 80s, and now he says, 'if people ask me what the secret of my success is, I say two things; I've stayed healthy and I've stayed married, so I have a base of serenity and my wife provides that. I've never seen myself as a writer first – a father first, second a husband, a family man. No marriage is smooth all the time; mine has been a terrific source of creative refreshment.'

Have fun

Some psychologists argue that the constant pressure on all of us to win and keep on winning is doing more harm than good. Children are tested and graded from the age of five, while the current generation of university students have never been so stressed out. Failure is not an option.

In America, one prominent academic, Harry Lewis, Dean of Harvard's undergraduate college, was so worried by his students' growing need to impress that he wrote a letter to parents headed, 'Slow Down: getting more out of Harvard by doing less'. Lewis said he had warned his students: 'You may balance your life better if you participate in some activities purely for fun. Many of the most important and rewarding things that you will do will be recorded on no piece of paper you take with you, but only as imprints on your mind and your soul.'

THE WORK

1 See failure as being due to factors that you can change. These factors may lie in yourself, the outside world, or in other people. Replace the word 'failure' with 'learning curve'. Identify what went wrong ➤

➤ and rectify the situation as decisively and dynamically as possible. Learn your lessons fast and thoroughly so you don't repeat them.

2 Observe how others have dealt successfully with similar failures, rather than going over the failure with fellow sufferers. Learn from the mistakes of others. You can't live long enough to make them all yourself. Behind every remarkably successful person lie some fascinating failures.

3 Stop focusing on how terrible the problem is, and concentrate on the solution. The successful spend only 10% of their time thinking about their problems and 90% dwelling on solutions. Become a master of solutions and options. You are never stuck and you always have choices. Ensure that you see them all by searching them out, because even if you don't spot them, they're there.

4 Remember, if you never experience failure, you are probably not trying to extend your boundaries enough. Keeping life interesting, staying fresh and involved has to include change and all change ➤

➤ involves some risk. You don't have to be reckless but attempting something new and different will ward off stagnation and smugness. And, doing this regardless of the outcome is the real challenge and bonus.

5 Define yourself clearly. How do you want to see yourself? Envisage yourself as the dynamic, attractive, personable person you would like to be, or whatever way you prefer to see yourself. Have a picture of yourself in mind and mould yourself into this shape. Always have in mind examples of the type of person you are emulating. Reinforce your persona by using sentences such as, 'I'm the sort of person who ...' and 'I'm not the sort of person who ...'

Moral: Practise self-belief as a way of life. When you need it most and it's lacking, practise it anyway. Don't wait for it to arrive before making your move.

FIONA HARROLD

Fiona Harrold's earliest exposure to coaching was at the age of eleven when, growing up in Northern Ireland, her beloved father would inspire her with the likes of Norman Vincent Peale, Napoleon Hill and Dale Carnegie.

Fiona's intention is to take the principles of personal responsibility, individual self-help and mutual support to the widest public through her books, workshops and website services: her website receives in excess of 500,000 visitors each month.

She is the author of the best-selling *Be Your Own Life Coach* (Hodder Mobius, £6.99), *The 10-Minute Life Coach* (Hodder Mobius, £6.99), *Reinvent Yourself* (Piatkus, £4.99). The *7 Rules of Success* (Hodder Mobius) is published in September 2005.

She was recently named by *The Times* newspaper as one of the 'new gurus who have got inside our minds to fill society's spiritual void'. She lives in London with her teenage son. Visit her website at www.fionaharrold.com.

1

Who are you now?

It is never too late to be what you might have been.

GEORGE ELIOT

This is one of the most thrilling and important sentences you'll ever read. Memorise it. Think about it. Savour it. Digest it. Drop it deep into your psyche. Let this profound truth shape your life from this day forth. It contains within it all you ever need to know to stay fresh in life, to keep yourself young, open to life and to your own terrific, unlimited potential.

Mary Ann Evans said this over 150 years ago. She knew all about reinvention even then, in Victorian England, when she had to appear to be a man, George Eliot, in order to get her wonderful novels published. She fulfilled her childhood dream of writing fiction at the age of thirty-seven, when her first novel was published. Her finest work, *Middlemarch*, was published in 1871 when she was fifty-two – so she also knew about not giving up on herself. Thankfully, things have changed since then, but the urge to be the best that we can and being inventive along the way is perennial, as relevant today as it was then.

You are an ambitious person. You have an innate desire to be someone, to live a terrific life, make it all work, no regrets. I know this because you're here reading this right now, and because I've never met a single person who didn't fit this description. Certainly, I've met people who've given up on themselves, on life, who're resigned and are waiting to be rescued by fate, God, someone or something. Sometimes the something is death.

> **You have an innate desire to be someone.**

I've met lots of people who think life has been unfair to them, resenting other people's success instead of concentrating on their own. Overwhelming self-doubt and lack of confidence can prevent people from ever starting.

I've met other people whose politics and perspective simply don't allow them to have it all, to be happy and love life, because they're convinced they have to be miserable to change the world, or that perhaps they just don't deserve to be happy and have a wonderful life. I should know because I used to be one of these people! Whatever the situation, underneath it all is the same human desire to live a good life, to make it all work and to be the best *you* that you could possibly be. The fact that people suppress, thwart and deny that fundamental urge is another matter.

George Eliot had an incredible urge for life, a huge appetite to fulfil her potential and live a life of her own design. She earned her own living at a time when a good marriage was the route offered to and expected of ladies. She moved from the provincial Midlands of England to a place of her own in London's Chelsea. She was considered plain by conventional standards, yet had a racy love life, causing a scandal by living with a married man, her 'spiritual' husband for many years. After his death she married a man twenty years her junior, forty years old to her sixty. Thought by many to be rather serious, her regular salons were the hub of intellectual, Bohemian society at the time.

I want that same vibrancy and exuberance for you. I want you to feel excited about your life, yourself and what lies ahead for you. It doesn't matter in the slightest if you've become a little tired, even worn out. Never mind how jaded or downright cynical you may sometimes feel. In fact, everyone needs to take a good look at themselves now and then just to check that they're still happy with the person they've become or are turning into, and that life's challenges haven't left their mark in a negative way.

A SELECTION OF TITLES AVAILABLE FROM PIATKUS BOOKS

0 7499 2205 2	Positive Living	Vera Peiffer	£9.99
0 7499 2296 6	Inner Happiness	Vera Peiffer	£9.99
0 7499 2441 1	The Joy Diet	Martha Beck	£10.99
0 7499 1926 4	The Confidence to Be Yourself	Brian Roet	£9.99
0 7499 2553 1	When Success Is Not Enough	Adam Walker	£.99

How 2 Kill your
husband
  Kathy, Lette

  Eva Rice